A SPECIAL GIFT FOR

_____

from

_____

A Grandparent's *Legacy*

Your Life Story
in Your Own Words

www.jcountryman.com

ISBN 978-1-4041-1331-2

Designed by Koechel Peterson & Associates, Minneapolis, MN

Printed in the United States of America

18 19 20 21 22 BTL 17 16 15 14 13 12 11

Contents

Introduction

In January we think of new beginnings; in February of valentines, first dates, and first kisses. Does ever a June pass without thoughts of our own wedding day? Surely summer evokes backseat memories of seemingly unending trips to Grandma's house or the beach. And don't November and December bring to mind family traditions and celebrations held dearly through the years?

Like ivy on the garden trellis, our lives are inescapably entwined with the seasons and months of the year. That is why we have designed this grandparent's memory journal in a twelve-month format. Each month features twelve intriguing questions with space to write a personal answer. Questions explore family history, childhood memories, lighthearted incidents, cherished traditions, and the dreams and spiritual adventures encountered in a lifetime of living.

Whether you choose to complete the journal in a few days, weeks, or over the course of a year, the questions will take you on a journey through the times and seasons of your life. This makes a tangible family record to pass on as a gift to your children and grandchildren, a loving memoir of written words that are windows to a grandparent's heart.

No matter what your age, memory and reminiscence open a richer, fuller understanding of who you are as a family. Let this memory journal be a starting point—a door into discussing and sharing the unique qualities of your life. May A Grandparent's Legacy draw you closer to each other as you share the experiences of a lifetime.

Cherish all your happy moments:

they make a fine cushion for old age

BOOTH TARKINGTON

YOUR FULL GIVEN NAME

YOUR DATE OF BIRTH

YOUR PLACE OF BIRTH

YOUR MOTHER'S FULL NAME

the place and date of her birth

YOUR FATHER'S FULL NAME

the place and date of his birth

THE NAMES OF YOUR PATERNAL GRANDPARENTS

the places and dates of their births

THE NAMES OF YOUR MATERNAL GRANDPARENTS

the places and dates of their births

THE NAMES OF YOUR SIBLINGS

the places and dates of their births

THE DATE AND PLACE OF YOUR MARRIAGE

THE FULL GIVEN NAME OF YOUR SPOUSE

THE NAMES AND BIRTH DATES OF YOUR CHILDREN

THE NAMES AND BIRTH DATES OF YOUR GRANDCHILDREN

What is your Favorite?

FLOWER OR PLANT

PERFUME OR COLOGNE

COLOR

HYMN OR SONG

BOOK

AUTHOR

SCRIPTURE, SAYING OR QUOTATION

HOLIDAY

DESSERT

VACATION SPOT

TYPE OF FOOD

SPORT

LEISURE ACTIVITY

Your favorite photo.

January

What is a Grandparent?

They are warmth and cheer and

laughter—someone who does loving

things you think about long after.

AUTHOR UNKNOWN

15

WHAT WAS YOUR FAVORITE
PASTIME AS A CHILD?

WHAT GAMES DID YOU PLAY?

WHAT WAS YOUR FAVORITE DOLL OR TOY?

January

WHO GAVE YOU YOUR NAME AND WHY?

DID YOU HAVE A NICKNAME?

HOW DID YOU GET IT?

Describe your childhood home.

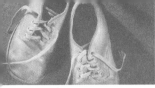

WHAT WAS THE SILLIEST THING YOU
EVER DID AS A CHILD?

WHAT WERE SUNDAYS LIKE AS A CHILD?

DID YOU GO TO CHURCH?

VISIT GRANDPARENTS?

WAS THERE A BIG FAMILY DINNER?

January

WHERE DID YOUR FATHER GO TO WORK
EVERY DAY AND WHAT DID HE DO?

SHARE THE MOST WONDERFUL THING
ABOUT YOUR FATHER.

January

*How did
your mother
spend her
day? Did
she have a
job or do
volunteer
work
outside the
home?*

*Share
the most
wonderful
thing
about your
mother.*

WHAT WERE SOME OF YOUR FAVORITE
TREATS AS A CHILD?

HOW MUCH DID THEY COST?

DID YOU HAVE A FAVORITE BEDTIME STORY
OR A PRAYER THAT YOU SAID BEFORE YOU
WENT TO SLEEP?

WHO TUCKED YOU IN?

January

DESCRIBE THE DAY YOUR FIRST
CHILD WAS BORN.

January

DESCRIBE THE DAY YOUR FIRST
GRANDCHILD WAS BORN.

Describe your grandparents' houses. Did you visit them often?

Why or why not?

LIST ONE SPECIAL MEMORY ABOUT EACH
OF YOUR BROTHERS AND SISTERS.

RECALL FOR ME SOME OF THE MOST
IMPORTANT LESSONS YOU HAVE LEARNED
IN LIFE.

January

February

Grandparents hold our tiny

hands for just a little while . . .

but our hearts forever.

AUTHOR UNKNOWN

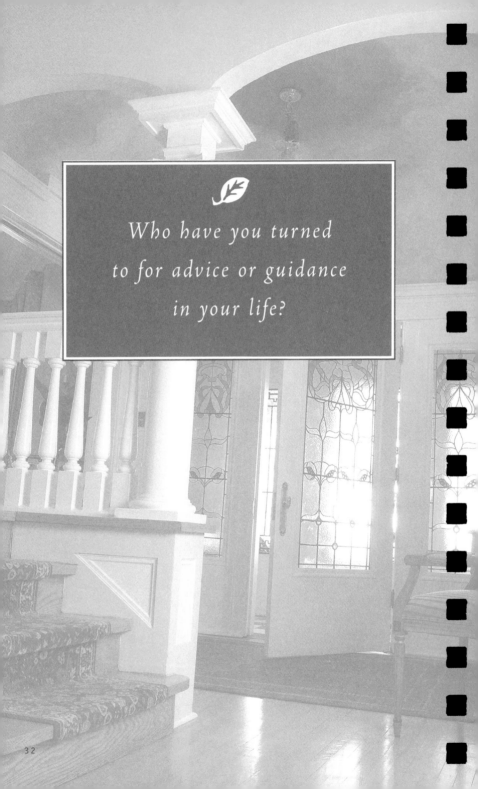

Who have you turned
to for advice or guidance
in your life?

February

AS A YOUNG CHILD, DID YOU PARTICIPATE
IN CHURCH, SCOUTING, OR SOME OTHER
ORGANIZATION OR ACTIVITY?

HOW IMPORTANT A ROLE DID THAT PLAY
IN YOUR LIFE?

DO YOU REMEMBER A SPECIAL BIBLE OR
STORYBOOK FROM YOUR CHILDHOOD?

WHO GAVE IT TO YOU?

DO YOU STILL HAVE IT?

DESCRIBE A MEMORABLE VALENTINE
YOU RECEIVED.

DESCRIBE A MEMORABLE VALENTINE YOU
GAVE TO SOMEONE.

HOW FAR DID YOU HAVE TO TRAVEL TO ATTEND ELEMENTARY SCHOOL AND HIGH SCHOOL, AND HOW DID YOU GET THERE?

February

What scent or sound immediately takes you back to childhood?

Describe the feeling it evokes.

WHAT WAS THE NAME OF YOUR
FAVORITE PET?

WHY WAS IT YOUR FAVORITE?

SHARE SOME NAMES OF OTHER PETS YOU
HAD GROWING UP.

WHAT CHORES DID YOU HAVE TO DO WHEN
YOU WERE GROWING UP?

DID YOU GET AN ALLOWANCE?

HOW MUCH WAS IT?

February

TELL ME ABOUT YOUR FIRST JOB.

Share your
favorite
memory
of each
of your
children.

March

Youth lives on hope,

old age on remembrance.

Can you recall a surprise visit
from family or friends?

March

WHAT DID YOU WANT TO BE WHEN
YOU GREW UP?

DID THAT CHANGE OVER THE YEARS?

WHAT WAS YOUR FAVORITE SUBJECT IN
ELEMENTARY SCHOOL?

IN HIGH SCHOOL?

WHO WAS YOUR ALL-TIME FAVORITE
TEACHER? WHY?

DESCRIBE ONE OF YOUR FAVORITE
DRESS-UP OUTFITS AS A CHILD. ON
WHAT OCCASIONS WOULD YOU WEAR IT?

March

DID YOU EVER HAVE A SPECIAL HIDEAWAY
OR PLAYHOUSE?

March

WHAT MADE IT SPECIAL?

What extracurricular activities were you involved in during high school?

Why did you choose those activities?

WHAT SPECIAL SONG OR SAYING DID YOU
ENJOY TEACHING YOUR CHILDREN AND
GRANDCHILDREN?

WHEN DID YOU HAVE Y
TELL ME ABOUT IT.   DATE?

March

ABOUT YOUR

WHAT DO YO

FIRST KISS?

L ME ABOUT YOUR FIRST LOVE.

March

What did you do to celebrate birthdays when you were growing up?

April

The simplest toy, one which

even the youngest child can operate,

is called a grandparent.

SAM LEVENSON

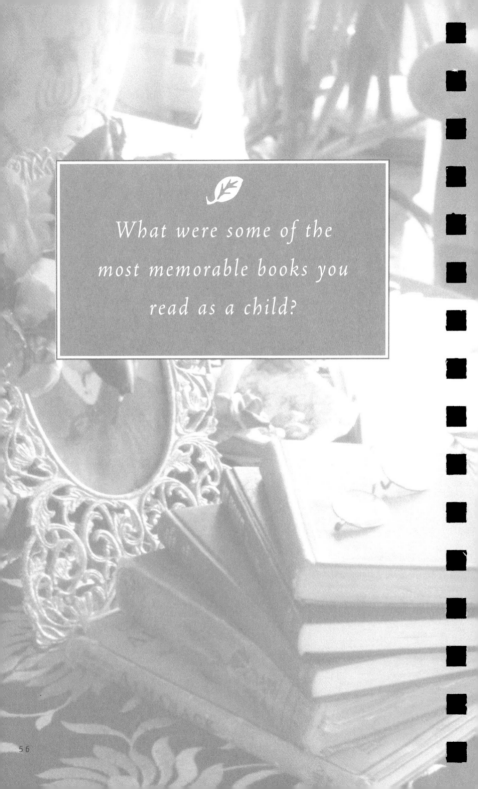

What were some of the most memorable books you read as a child?

April

TELL ABOUT AN AWARD OR SPECIAL
RECOGNITION YOU HAVE RECEIVED.

WHAT WERE YOUR FAMILY FINANCES
LIKE WHEN YOU WERE GROWING UP?

HOW DID THAT AFFECT YOU?

WHAT MISCHIEVOUS CHILDHOOD EXPERIENCE DO YOU REMEMBER MOST?

April

WHAT MEANINGFUL ADVICE DID YOU
RECEIVE FROM AN ADULT?

WHAT WERE THE CIRCUMSTANCES?

What similarities do you see in your children and your grandchildren?

WHAT THINGS DO YOU WISH YOU HAD
DONE IN CHILDHOOD OR ADOLESCENCE?

WHAT ARE THE THINGS YOU ARE MOST GLAD YOU TRIED?

April

DESCRIBE YOUR MOTHER IN
HER BEST DRESS.

WHAT SIMILARITIES WITH YOUR
MOTHER DO YOU NOW SEE IN YOURSELF
OR IN YOUR CHILDREN?

April

Describe your father in his working clothes.

What similarities with your father do you now see in yourself or in your children?

WHAT DID YOU LIKE TO DO BEST WITH YOUR CHILDHOOD FRIENDS?

SHARE SOME FAVORITE GOODIES YOU
LOVE TO HAVE AT YOUR HOUSE WHEN
COMPANY ARRIVES.

May

To keep the heart unwrinkled,

to be hopeful, kindly, cheerful,

reverent – that is to triumph over old age.

THOMAS BAILEY ALDRICH

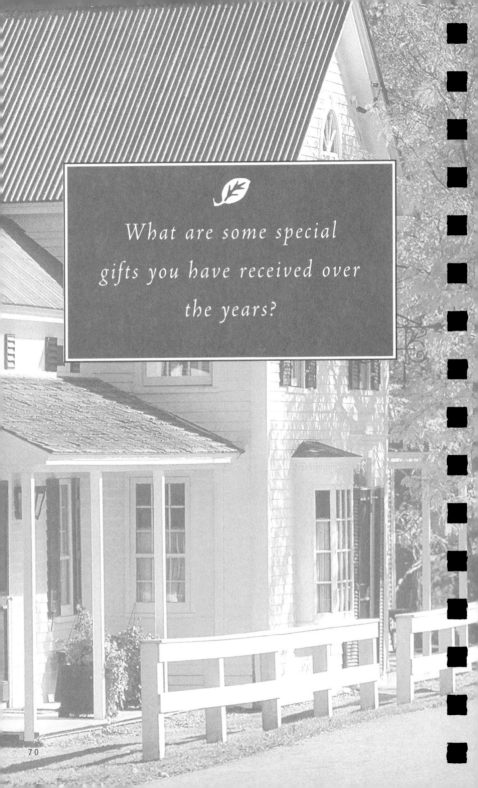

What are some special
gifts you have received over
the years?

May

WHAT FAMILY TRADITIONS DO
YOU WANT TO PASS ON TO YOUR
GRANDCHILDREN?

WHAT IS ONE OF THE MOST DIFFICULT
CHOICES YOU EVER HAD TO MAKE?

WOULD YOU MAKE THAT SAME
CHOICE AGAIN?

DID YOU EVER GO TO A DANCE?

TELL ME ABOUT IT.

May

WHAT KIND OF CAR DID YOUR
FAMILY DRIVE?

WERE YOU PROUD OF IT OR
EMBARRASSED BY IT?

Did you
attend
family
reunions?

Share a
memory
of one.

WHAT IS YOUR FAVORITE SEASON OF THE YEAR? WHY?

RECALL A MEMORABLE FIRST DAY OF
SCHOOL FOR ONE OF YOUR CHILDREN.

May

TELL ME ABOUT YOUR BEST CHILDHOOD FRIEND.

May

If you went to college or to a career training school, where did you go and why?

DESCRIBE THE BEST JOB AND THE WORST
JOB YOU HAD IN YOUR YOUNGER DAYS.

WHAT WERE YOUR YOUTHFUL GOALS
AND AMBITIONS FOR LIFE?

WHICH ONES HAVE YOU BEEN ABLE
TO FULFILL?

May

ARE THERE CERTAIN SCRIPTURES
OR OTHER WRITINGS THAT YOU
REPEATEDLY TURN TO FOR
INSPIRATION AND GUIDANCE?

May

*Did you
ever meet
someone
famous?*

*Describe
the event
and your
reaction.*

June

Few things are more delightful than

grandchildren fighting over your lap.

DOUG LARSON

If you learned to play a musical instrument, tell me about your memories of lessons, practice, recitals, and your music teacher. If not, what instrument did you always want to play and why?

June

HOW OLD WERE YOU WHEN YOU MET
YOUR SPOUSE, AND WHAT ATTRACTED
YOU TO THAT PERSON?

WHEN DID YOU FIRST KNOW YOU
WANTED TO GET MARRIED? TELL ME
ABOUT THE PROPOSAL.

WHAT DID YOU WEAR ON YOUR
WEDDING DAY? WHAT DID YOUR
FUTURE SPOUSE WEAR?

SHARE A TRADITION FROM YOUR
COURTSHIP THAT STILL REMAINS SPECIAL.

TELL ME ABOUT YOUR WEDDING DAY,
FROM BEGINNING TO END.

June

*Where did
you go
on your
honeymoon?*

*Share one
humorous
incident.*

WHAT WAS YOUR FIRST HOUSE OR
APARTMENT TOGETHER LIKE?

WHAT HUMOROUS MOMENTS DO YOU RECALL FROM YOUR WEDDING DAY?

June

WHAT DO YOU LOVE BEST ABOUT YOUR MATE NOW?

June

Tell me about an anniversary celebration that was very special.

July

And in the end, it's not the

years in your life that count.

It's the life in your years.

ABRAHAM LINCOLN

Share a family tradition
or memory from the
Fourth of July.

July

HAVE YOU EVER PARTICIPATED IN A
RALLY OR DEMONSTRATION?

WHAT WAS THE CAUSE?

SHARE YOUR FEELINGS ABOUT IT.

WHO IN YOUR FAMILY SERVED IN THE
MILITARY AND WHEN?

DO YOU HAVE A SPECIAL MEMORY OF
SOMEONE?

DID YOU LEARN TO SWIM?

AT WHAT AGE?

HOW?

July

DID YOU TAKE FAMILY VACATIONS WHEN
GROWING UP? RECORD ONE MEMORABLE
EXPERIENCE.

Tell about your first trip by plane, train, or ship. How old were you?

Share your feelings about the experience.

IF YOU EVER TRAVELED ABROAD, WHAT
WAS THE MOST UNIQUE EXPERIENCE
OF THE TRIP? IF NOT, WHAT COUNTRY
WOULD YOU MOST LIKE TO VISIT? WHY?

DESCRIBE THE MOST FASCINATING PLACE YOU HAVE VISITED.

July

TELL ABOUT A DRIVING TRIP WITH YOUR CHILDREN.

July

Did your relatives come to visit in the summer, or did you go to visit them?

What are your memories of those visits?

HOW DID YOU LEARN TO DRIVE?

DESCRIBE YOUR FIRST CAR.

DID A TRAGEDY EVERY STRIKE
YOUR FAMILY? _____

HOW WERE YOU AFFECTED? _____

July

August

No cowboy was ever faster on

the draw than a grandparent

pulling a baby picture out of a wallet.

AUTHOR UNKNOWN

What one special quality
do you see in each of your
children and grandchildren?

August

DID YOU HAVE A COLLECTION WHEN
YOU WERE GROWING UP?

WHAT INITIALLY SPARKED YOUR
INTEREST IN IT?

DESCRIBE A PERFECT SUMMER DAY.

WHAT KIND OF OUTDOOR WORK DO YOU LIKE? WHY?

August

WHEN DID YOU LEARN HOW TO RIDE
A BIKE, OR TO WATER SKI, SNOW SKI,
ROLLER SKATE, OR SAIL?

SHARE YOUR MEMORIES OF THE
EXPERIENCE.

August

What summer games and activities did your family enjoy?

117

DID YOU EVER MILK A COW OR SPEND
TIME ON A FARM OR IN THE COUNTRY?
TELL ME ABOUT IT.

DESCRIBE YOUR FIRST TRIP ALONE.

August

WHAT PLACES WOULD YOU STILL LIKE TO VISIT? WHY?

August

Describe a frightening or difficult experience from childhood.

121

TELL ME ABOUT YOUR MOST
UNFORGETTABLE SUMMER EXPERIENCE
AS A CHILD. ⎯⎯⎯⎯⎯⎯⎯⎯⎯⎯⎯⎯⎯⎯⎯⎯

LIST SOME OF YOUR FAVORITE PLACES
TO GO ON VACATION.

August

September

Example is a lesson that all can read.

GILBERT WEST

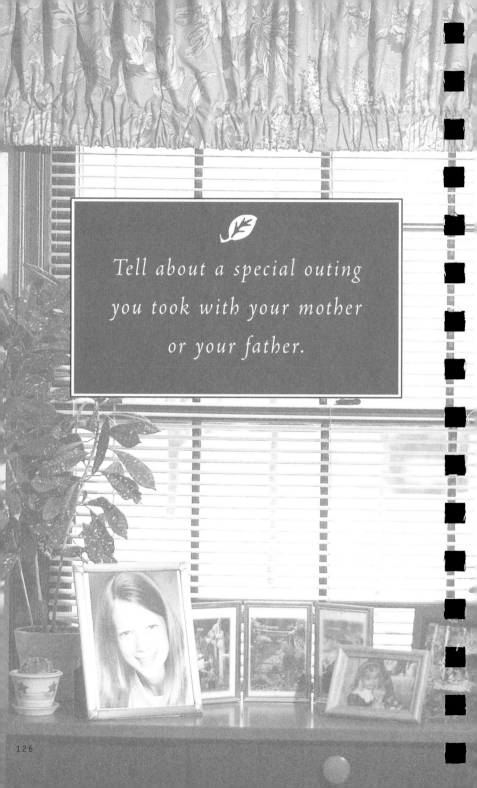

Tell about a special outing
you took with your mother
or your father.

September

WHAT WAS THE MOST TENDER DAY IN
YOUR CHILDHOOD?

WHAT WAS THE MOST TENDER DAY
AS A PARENT?

SHARE SOME FAMILY RITUALS WHEN
GETTING READY TO GO BACK TO
SCHOOL.

AS A YOUNG PERSON, DID YOU
VOLUNTEER FOR WORK IN CHURCH OR
THE COMMUNITY?

TELL ME ABOUT IT.

September

WHEN DID YOU MOVE AWAY FROM HOME?

DESCRIBE WHERE YOU LIVED AND HOW
YOU FELT ABOUT IT.

September

Who was your best friend after you were married?

Describe some of the fun things you did together.

DESCRIBE THE TIME WHEN YOU
OR YOUR OLDEST SIBLING MOVED
AWAY FROM HOME.

HOW DID IT AFFECT THE REST OF
THE FAMILY?

WHAT SPECIAL TALENTS DID YOUR
PARENTS NURTURE IN YOU?

HOW HAVE YOU DEVELOPED THOSE
TALENTS?

September

WHAT SPECIAL TALENTS DID YOU NURTURE IN YOUR OWN CHILDREN?

September

What is something you learned from an especially happy time in your life?

WHAT WOULD YOU LIKE TO LEARN TO DO?

_____

_____

_____

_____

_____

_____

WHY? _____

_____

_____

_____

_____

_____

_____

_____

_____

_____

WHAT WOULD YOU DO DIFFERENTLY IN
LIFE IF YOU COULD?

WHAT WOULD YOU DO DIFFERENTLY IN
PARENTING IF YOU COULD?

September

DESCRIBE THE MOST SIGNIFICANT EVENT YOU HAVE EVER ATTENDED.

September

Share a
favorite
poem or
a passage
of writing
that has
been
especially
meaningful
in your
life.

October

A grandmother pretends she doesn't

know who you are on Halloween.

ERMA BOMBECK

What do you like best about

being a grandparent? Why?

142

October

HOW WOULD YOU LIKE TO BE REMEMBERED?

WHY IS THIS IMPORTANT TO YOU?

WHAT ARE SOME OF THE THINGS THAT
YOUR GRANDCHILDREN DO THAT MAKE
YOU SMILE?

WHAT DO YOU CONSIDER TO BE SOME OF LIFE'S MOST DIFFICULT CHALLENGES?

October

WHAT DO YOU CONSIDER TO BE LIFE'S GREATEST GIFTS?

October

What responsibilities did your parents require of you as a child?

Explain how this affected your growth and development.

WHEN AND WHERE DID YOU BUY YOUR FIRST HOUSE?

DESCRIBE THE HOUSE AND EXPLAIN
ANY SIGNIFICANCE IT HELD FOR YOU.

October

WHAT IS THE STRANGEST THING YOU HAVE EVER SEEN?

October

Name your favorite hobby. When and where did you start doing it?

Why do you enjoy doing it?

TELL ABOUT A MEMORABLE HOTEL OR
RESORT YOU HAVE VISITED. DESCRIBE
THE LOCATION AND THE SIGNIFICANCE
OF THE VISIT.

DID YOU EVER GO ON A HAYRIDE OR BOB
FOR APPLES?

WHAT OTHER FUN FALL ACTIVITIES DID
YOU AND YOUR FRIENDS ENJOY?

October

November

A candle loses nothing by lighting

another candle.

AUTHOR UNKNOWN

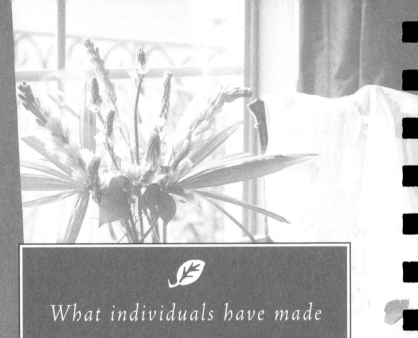

What individuals have made the greatest impact on your life? In what way?

November

WHAT IS YOUR MOST TREASURED
POSSESSION AND WHY?

WHO WERE YOUR ROLE MODELS WHEN
YOU WERE GROWING UP? ⎯⎯⎯⎯⎯⎯⎯

⎯⎯⎯⎯⎯⎯⎯⎯⎯⎯⎯⎯⎯⎯⎯⎯⎯⎯⎯⎯⎯⎯⎯

⎯⎯⎯⎯⎯⎯⎯⎯⎯⎯⎯⎯⎯⎯⎯⎯⎯⎯⎯⎯⎯⎯⎯

⎯⎯⎯⎯⎯⎯⎯⎯⎯⎯⎯⎯⎯⎯⎯⎯⎯⎯⎯⎯⎯⎯⎯

⎯⎯⎯⎯⎯⎯⎯⎯⎯⎯⎯⎯⎯⎯⎯⎯⎯⎯⎯⎯⎯⎯⎯

HOW HAVE THEY SHAPED YOU
AS A PERSON? ⎯⎯⎯⎯⎯⎯⎯⎯⎯⎯⎯⎯

⎯⎯⎯⎯⎯⎯⎯⎯⎯⎯⎯⎯⎯⎯⎯⎯⎯⎯⎯⎯⎯⎯⎯

⎯⎯⎯⎯⎯⎯⎯⎯⎯⎯⎯⎯⎯⎯⎯⎯⎯⎯⎯⎯⎯⎯⎯

⎯⎯⎯⎯⎯⎯⎯⎯⎯⎯⎯⎯⎯⎯⎯⎯⎯⎯⎯⎯⎯⎯⎯

⎯⎯⎯⎯⎯⎯⎯⎯⎯⎯⎯⎯⎯⎯⎯⎯⎯⎯⎯⎯⎯⎯⎯

⎯⎯⎯⎯⎯⎯⎯⎯⎯⎯⎯⎯⎯⎯⎯⎯⎯⎯⎯⎯⎯⎯⎯

⎯⎯⎯⎯⎯⎯⎯⎯⎯⎯⎯⎯⎯⎯⎯⎯⎯⎯⎯⎯⎯⎯⎯

⎯⎯⎯⎯⎯⎯⎯⎯⎯⎯⎯⎯⎯⎯⎯⎯⎯⎯⎯⎯⎯⎯⎯

WHAT IS YOUR MOST VIVID MEMORY OF BEING A NEW PARENT?

November

HOW DID YOU CHOOSE YOUR
CHILDREN'S NAMES?

November

What family
name has
been passed
down
to other
generations?

Any
nicknames
that have
been passed
down?

WHAT WAS A FAVORITE THANKSGIVING
TRADITION IN YOUR FAMILY?

WHAT ARE SOME THINGS FROM
YOUR CHILDHOOD THAT YOU ARE
THANKFUL FOR?

November

WHAT CHILDHOOD MEMORY FIRST
COMES TO YOUR MIND WHEN YOU
THINK ABOUT WINTER?

November

What is your most poignant memory about the childhood of your own children?

WHAT ARE SOME OF THE THINGS
YOU REMEMBER MOST ABOUT YOUR
CHILDHOOD FRIENDS?

WHICH OF THOSE FRIENDS STILL
REMAIN CLOSE TODAY?

WHAT FAMILY RECIPE WOULD YOU LIKE
TO PASS ON TO YOUR CHILDREN AND
GRANDCHILDREN?

November

WHAT NEW TRADITION WOULD
YOU LIKE TO START IN THE FAMILY
WITH THE GRANDCHILDREN?

WHAT IS ITS SIGNIFICANCE?

November

Share a favorite holiday food from your childhood days.

December

Grandmas are moms

with lots of frosting.

AUTHOR UNKNOWN

Tell about some Christmas
rituals in your family and
how you felt about them.

December

WERE YOU EVER IN A CHRISTMAS
PROGRAM OR CHRISTMAS PARADE?

TELL ABOUT THAT EXPERIENCE.

WHAT FAVORITE CHRISTMAS TREASURES HAVE YOU KEPT FROM YEAR TO YEAR?

SHARE THEIR ORIGINS.

December

Tell about a memorable Christmas visit with relatives.

WHAT IS YOUR FAVORITE CHRISTMAS CAROL? WHY?

DID YOU HAVE A CHRISTMAS STOCKING AS
A CHILD, OR A SPECIAL ORNAMENT? WHAT
DID IT LOOK LIKE?

WHAT IS THE FIRST CHRISTMAS GIFT YOU
REMEMBER RECEIVING?

December

DESCRIBE THE CHRISTMAS THAT HAS
BEEN THE MOST MEANINGFUL TO YOU
AS A PARENT AND AS A GRANDPARENT.

December

What would be the most wonderful gift you could receive?

Why?

WHAT IS SOMETHING THAT YOU AND
YOUR MATE ENJOY DOING TOGETHER?

_____

_____

_____

_____

_____

_____

_____

_____

_____

_____

_____

_____

_____

_____

WHAT WOULD YOU LIKE TO SEE HAPPEN IN YOUR LIFE IN THE NEXT TEN YEARS?

December

DID YOU EVER SURPRISE SOMEONE ELSE
WITH A GOOD DEED OR GIFT? DESCRIBE
WHAT HAPPENED.

DID YOU EVER GET SURPRISED BY
SOMEONE, MAYBE FOR YOUR BIRTHDAY
OR ANNIVERSARY?

December

What word best describes your life?

Explain why.

WHAT ADVICE ABOUT LIFE DO YOU WANT
ALL OF YOUR FAMILY TO REMEMBER?

TELL ABOUT A SIGNIFICANT ILLNESS YOU OR SOMEONE IN YOUR FAMILY FACED?

December

Special Memories

Use the following pages to share special
family stories, words of wisdom, more
stories about yourself, or words of love
you would like to be passed down to your
children and grandchildren.

Photos

Photos